IMAGES
of America

BAYVILLE

The village of Bayville shares borders with Locust Valley on the west; Mill Neck Creek, Oyster Bay Harbor, and the village of Mill Neck on the south; Centre Island on the east; and the Long Island Sound on the north. This 1873 map shows the homesteads of the village. (Courtesy of Oyster Bay Historical Society.)

On the cover: In 1920, automobiles and passengers were ferried between Bayville and Stamford, Connecticut, from Ferry Beach. This was the shortest way to travel to Connecticut and beyond for residents of Bayville and the surrounding towns. The dock was located just west of the present Crescent Beach Club. Service was suspended in 1937 with the opening of the Whitestone Bridge. (Courtesy of Bayville Historical Museum.)

IMAGES
of America

BAYVILLE

The Incorporated Village of Bayville

ARCADIA
PUBLISHING

Published by Arcadia Publishing
Charleston, South Carolina

Library of Congress Control Number: 2009922891

For all general information contact Arcadia Publishing at:
Telephone 843-853-2070
Fax 843-853-0044
E-mail sales@arcadiapublishing.com
For customer service and orders:
Toll-Free 1-888-313-2665

Visit us on the Internet at www.arcadiapublishing.com

Dedicated to the residents who make up this special community.

CONTENTS

ACKNOWLEDGMENTS

On the occasion of the 90th anniversary of the incorporation of the village of Bayville, Mayor Victoria Siegel and the members of the village board gratefully acknowledge the effort and dedication of the individuals who donated their time and painstakingly researched, organized, and developed this tribute to the village and the residents who inhabit this wonderful community. Many people were directly involved in this endeavor; however, the driving force of this publication was Angela Monte of Lattingtown, who was skillfully assisted by David and Catherine Rapelje, Deborah Tyler, and John G. Kennedy of Bayville.

A special thanks goes to John E. Hammond, town of Oyster Bay historian, for his help. Thank you to all the individuals, too numerous to list, who shared photographs from their personal collections.

Other photographs are courtesy of the following institutions: Bayville Historical Museum, Garvies Point Museum and Preserve, the Heather Bredberg collection, Huntington Historical Society, Metropolitan Transportation Authority, NavSource Online, Oyster Bay Historical Society, and Photo Archive Center of Nassau County.

INTRODUCTION

The village of Bayville is a small hamlet located on the north shore of Nassau County, overlooking Long Island Sound. Several thousand years ago, glaciers deposited the rocks and soil that represent the geological makeup of this area and the surrounding villages, towns, and cities. This beautiful community boasts picturesque cliffs that overlook the sound, panoramic water views of Connecticut, and sandy beaches for all to enjoy. Originally incorporated in 1919, Bayville celebrates its 90th year as an incorporated village in 2009.

The history of Bayville began in 1658, when, with the permission of the Crown of England, the land was purchased from the Matinecock Indian tribe by Daniel Whitehead, an Oyster Bay settler. A few years later, the land was divided into lots and sold to be used as pastures because the natural water boundaries provided a secure location for grazing animals. In 1754, a road, now known as Bayville Avenue, was surveyed from Beaver Swamp through Bayville to Centre Island, becoming the main route through the area for many years.

Throughout the years, various industries thrived in Bayville, among them shellfish harvesting, sand and gravel mining, and asparagus farming. Over a period of time, mining operations and asparagus farming gave way to Bayville becoming a summer resort and playground for vacationers from the surrounding area. Today only the shellfish industry, which in the early days was the major source of income, has survived, mainly through the efforts of Frank M. Flowers and Sons, which in 1887 began harvesting oysters in Oyster Bay Harbor. At the present time, the company is still mainly involved with the production of oysters through an intricate method of greenhouse cultivation.

At the dawn of the 19th century, Bayville was becoming a popular summer community and resort destination. One popular attraction located opposite Oak Neck Beach was a casino that housed a roller-skating rink, dining room, and dance hall. Residences included summer homes and beach cottages as well as magnificent estates with beautiful rolling lawns and gardens; one even had its own nine-hole golf course. The construction of these homes and mansions brought a wave of new faces, including immigrants from Europe, tradesmen, and household help, which significantly increased the local population. Today one can still find ancestors of those original families living in and around the Bayville area.

Perhaps the most recognizable symbol of the village of Bayville is the bridge that connects the east end of Bayville to Mill Neck. The construction of the first bridge in 1898, at a cost of about $5,000, shortened the route to Oyster Bay, which had been either through Mill Neck or across the harbor by a water taxi that operated on weekends. Over the years, there have been four bridges constructed or renovated between Bayville and Mill Neck to ease the traffic flow and provide direct access to the Oyster Bay area. Since the bridge is the first image of the Bayville peninsula seen by residents or travelers returning from Oyster Bay, this icon remains a welcome sight for many as they approach the area.

Ferry service from Bayville to New York City and Stamford, Connecticut, was available to residents and tourists alike. In 1917, the Wenck Marine Corporation offered regular daily crossings from Ferry Beach in Bayville to both Rye and Stamford. Traveling across Long Island Sound provided passengers with breathtaking views of both coasts and the surrounding area. Additional ferry transportation provided service to New York and was based at Steamboat Wharf in Bayville. However, in 1937, shortly after the opening of the Whitestone Bridge, water transportation across the Long Island Sound to Stamford was discontinued.

Typically the Bayville community mirrors countless small towns and cities located throughout the country that provide a superb environment in which to dwell and raise a family. Life in and around the area supports the enthusiasm generated by the younger generation, wherein participation in all kinds of sports and learning activities takes a primary role in personal development and family pride. In fact, today's residents are proud to boast that they and their families live, play, and thrive in Bayville.

As the younger generation matures, obtains a higher education, marries, and conceivably relocates to similar areas throughout the country, one can be sure that the essential foundation of life as it was experienced in Bayville remains the guiding light to enduring happiness. Those values, as basic as they may seem, involve the establishment of intricate foundations that support friendships that are nurtured for a lifetime. They may be as simple as Little League sports or as complex as high school physics, but they are all a part of life's experiences that are shared with friends and acquaintances.

By almost any measure, Bayville is typical of all those expectations as the residents are delighted to preserve their history, and yet they constantly seek to enhance the future for themselves and their families. Moreover, this picturesque village is uniquely situated within a relatively close drive to New York City, which offers a myriad of resources of the world's finest cultural events and related excitement to visitors from around the globe. Therefore, Bayville residents enjoy the best of both worlds: the solitude of a relatively small village and the unsurpassed excitement of one of the world's major cities.

Contained in this publication are a series of historic images, taken over a period of time, involving the residents, their way of life, and the extraordinary growth of the village of Bayville. The work that was involved in preparing this publication was complex to say the least and a credit to the investigative ability of the researchers involved. Therefore, it is the wish of the committee producing this periodical that its contents will be informative and relate to the development of a truly wonderful community.

—John G. Kennedy

One

EARLY DAYS

Life on and around the water has changed through the years. For early settlers, the water offered an abundance of food, land was farmed, and life was simple. Today it is the home to over 7,000 residents. It is a part of everyone's memories of days spent in Bayville. Idyllic, peaceful days spent on the water surrounding this tranquil village were and still are a favorite pastime for many residents.

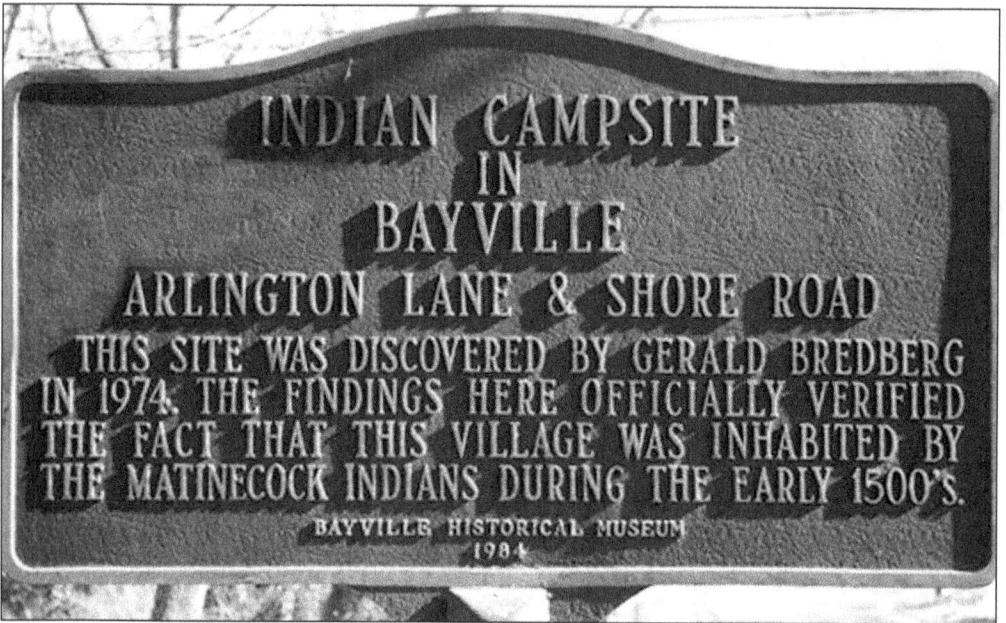

INDIAN CAMPSITE
IN
BAYVILLE
ARLINGTON LANE & SHORE ROAD
THIS SITE WAS DISCOVERED BY GERALD BREDBERG
IN 1974. THE FINDINGS HERE OFFICIALLY VERIFIED
THE FACT THAT THIS VILLAGE WAS INHABITED BY
THE MATINECOCK INDIANS DURING THE EARLY 1500'S.
BAYVILLE HISTORICAL MUSEUM
1984

It has been said that archaeologist Gerald Bredberg stumbled upon these skeletal remains by accident while he walked past a construction site. It was because of his keen eye and educated observations that he discovered and identified what to others appeared to be a piece of rock. This plaque was erected in 1984 by the Bayville Historical Museum and marks the exact location of the find.

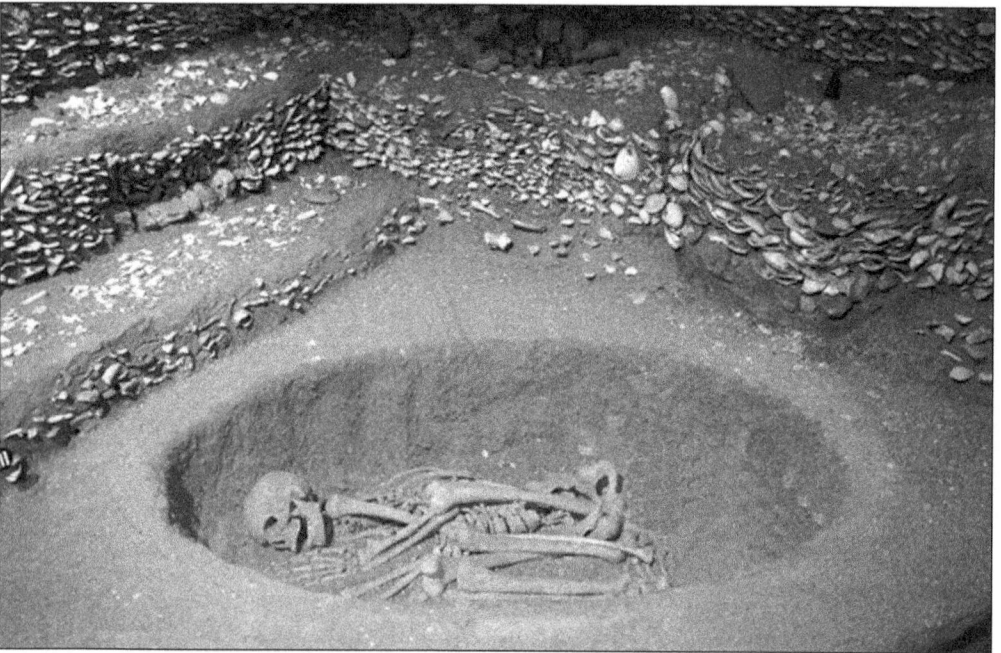

During a construction excavation in 1974, skeletal remains were found. Testing verified that they were Native American, dating back to the 1500s. Pictured is a replica of a Native American burial site. Shells visible in the earth are evidence of the abundance of shellfish, which were a staple of the Native American diet.

This Native American pottery was found at an unidentified site in Bayville. According to the marking, it is believed to date back to the 1500s.

In this three-dimensional display, the viewer is able to see what Native American life may have been like in Bayville. Shellfish was an abundant source of food as were fish and small game. A protected harbor and creek made it an ideal camping ground for the early Native American tribe believed to be the Matinecock.

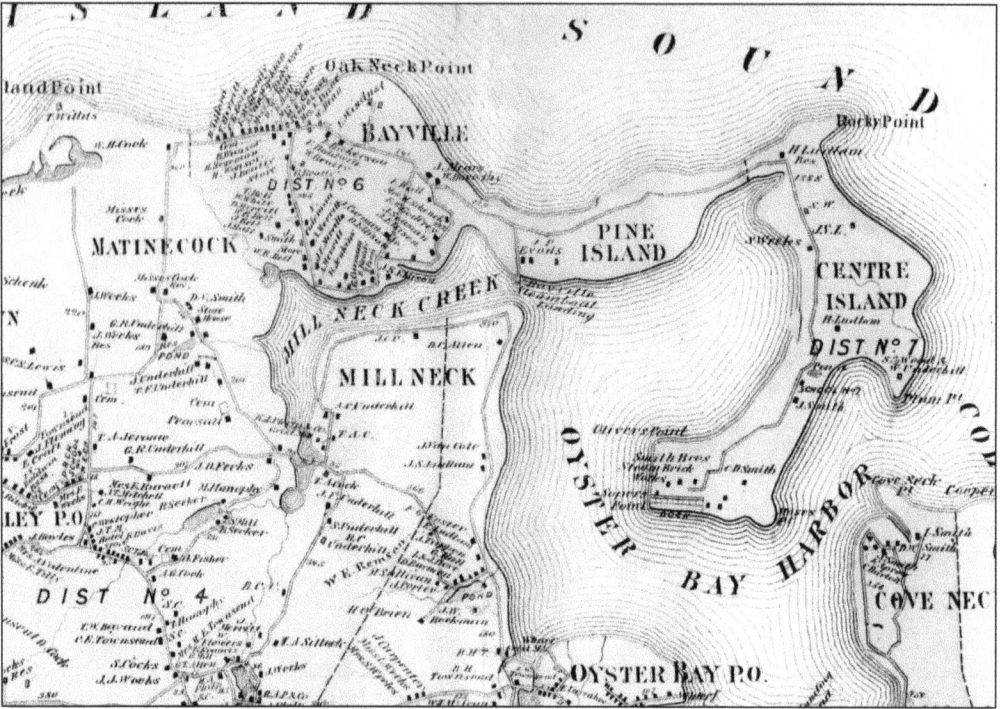

Many names that appear on this 1873 map are those of families that are still Bayville residents. It is also clear that there is no bridge connecting Mill Neck to Bayville but rather a steamboat landing dock.

Salt hay, as it is commonly known, is a species of marsh grass. Early settlers harvested the salt hay, which was used for insulating icehouses, packaging fragile items, and as bedding for livestock.

Members of the Ludlam family are seen in front of their home, which was located on Centre Island in what was called Mingo Springs. The property was located north of today's Seawanhaka Corinthian Yacht Club. In 1754, Charles Ludlam had the length of road surveyed from Beaver Swamp in Mill Neck to Mingo Springs. He played an important part in the history of Bayville, and years later, his name was immortalized when the road leading from the bridge to Bayville Avenue was named Ludlam Avenue.

The Ludlam family moved from their home on Centre Island to a home in Bayville, located at what is now the corner of Vivona Court and Ludlam Avenue. Some members of the Ludlam family are seen on the front porch of their house. The horse and carriage was the one of the most common modes of transportation at the time of this photograph. Here the Ludlam sisters are seen in the family carriage as they wait in front of their Bayville residence.

The Tilfords, one of the oldest families in Bayville, lived in this house built in 1890 on Locust Avenue. The family owned and operated the first blacksmith shop.

Situated on the southwest corner of Library Lane and Perry Avenue was the original Finnin family home. Having first purchased a store and market from the Beattys on Perry Avenue, the Finnins then opened a butcher shop on Library Lane. The horse-drawn market wagon delivering goods was a familiar sight for many years in the village.

Elizabeth Anne Merritt in the rocking chair and aunt Hettie Merritt Beatty in the hammock sit with the rest of the family in this 1890s photograph. The house was located on Klondike Lane and Lovers Lane, now Library Lane and Perry Avenue. The Merritt family, along with many of the original families, came from Connecticut and settled in Bayville and surrounding areas.

These early homesteads were south of Bayville Avenue near Perry Avenue. The original water tower can be seen on the right. The photograph was taken around 1906.

Looking east toward Centre Island at the intersection of Bayville and Ludlam Avenues is the area called the Pines. In the early 1900s, the automobile became a more common sight than the horse and carriage. With the bridge at the end of Ludlam Avenue, the town center started to shift from Oak Neck to the Pines. Real estate was being sold, praising the virtues of living in this community with an easy commute to Manhattan on the steamboat *Northport*, which departed from the new ferry dock located on the sound-side shoreline.

Horsing around in front of the ice-cream shop on Ludlam Avenue and Bayville Avenue on a hot summer day in 1903 from left to right are Will Blunt, Libbie Guindon, Steve Thorpe, and Adelaide D. Griffin.

"Uncle John and Uncle Will (on horse) plowing Dean Farm on the Sound (nine acres) by Merritt Lane" is how the caption on the back of this photograph reads. This is the same property that later became home to the Rouss mansion.

Newlywed Joseph Davis bought his bride this house at 7 Bell Lane, which he purchased from George Hall.

A Mr. Davis looks pensive while the rest of his family appears to be having fun as they gather for a family photograph on this summer afternoon on the family property.

The Tagliabue family had their home and boardinghouse on Cyprus Point in 1910. Members of the Tagliabue family still live in the home today, which is located at the end of Mountain Avenue on Mill Neck Creek.

Several generations of the Tagliabue family pose for a photograph on their property in 1910. Mill Neck Creek can be seen in the background.

In the 1920s, this family is seen enjoying a meal on their campsite at what is now Pleasant View Drive. Access to the beach was such that residents could load up their cars with all their camping gear and just drive down to the beach. Although this photograph was taken in the 1920s, the older ladies still preferred to wear these outdated long dresses.

Looking east along the western end of Bayville Avenue are many of the early homes of the villagers. The second house on the right belonged to the Winslow family.

The McCaffrey cottage was situated on Dickerson Avenue. John McCaffrey was mayor of Bayville from 1936 to 1948.

Lulu and Louis Valentine sit on the porch of their boathouse on Mill Neck Creek. Louis was the water district commissioner.

Two

ESTATES

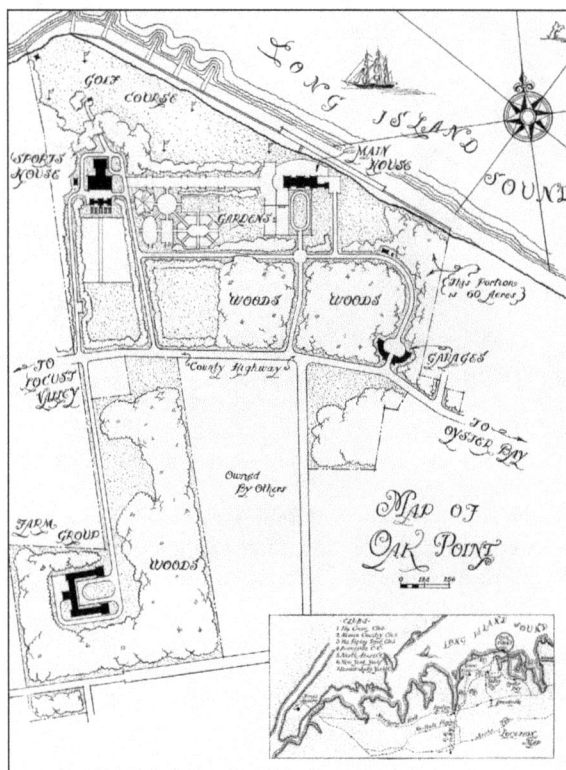

A map of Oak Point, the Harrison Williams estate, shows the nine-hole golf course that was on Long Island Sound and numerous buildings. These buildings included a tennis and pool house, guesthouse, stables, and garages. There were also magnificent gardens. Mona Williams sold all this property to a developer in the 1950s with the exception of 27 acres that she donated to the village.

A. Winslow Pierce, a corporate attorney who specialized in railroad law, became the first mayor of Bayville in 1919. Through his efforts, the village was incorporated. Pierce built his home on land owned by Stephen Van Cruger, who was a New York real estate speculator. In 1903, Pierce commissioned the firm of Babb, Cook and Willard to build his mansion. It was called Dunstable, located on Oak Neck. The Pierce family lived there until the 1920s, when the property was sold to Harrison Williams. Pierce lived in Bayville until his death in 1938.

Mona Travis Strader Schlesinger Bush had already been married twice before becoming engaged to Williams. Known as a fashion icon, she was a socialite with a passion for antiques and art. Her likeness was once featured as part of a cover design for the *New Yorker* magazine.

Oak Point, Harrison and Mona Williams's estate, was purchased from A. Winslow Pierce. In 1926, his fortune was estimated to be $600 million, which he made owning public utilities. Mona was named one of the best-dressed women in America. Besides Oak Point, the Williams family also owned homes on Fifth Avenue, in Palm Beach, Florida, and a villa overlooking Capri, Italy.

To enter Oak Point, visitors passed between two gatehouses before driving up the long, gravel, tree-lined driveway to the main house.

The indoor tennis court and pool house on the Harrison Williams estate exemplified the lifestyle of the very wealthy. They were connected by a lounge, a men's dressing room, a women's dressing room, and washrooms. The lounge overlooked the tennis courts so spectators could watch tennis matches from an elevated platform. In later years, the empty structures were destroyed by a fire that was battled by the Bayville Fire Company assisted by neighboring fire companies.

```
                    BALENCIAGA
                   IO, AVENUE GEORGE V
                          PARIS

                                    Paris, le 26 Novembre 1956.

        Mt.

Madame la Comtesse de BISMARCK - Oak Point Dayville Long Island NEW YO
Passeport Nº 364.542.-

                    REPORT..........................  3.205.000.--
Octobre    I2 √ Modèle 69 - Tailleur de lainage noir.........  I50.000.--
            √ Modèle 23 - Tailleur de tweed gris............  I75.000.--
            √ Modèle 42 - Tailleur de lainage gris.........  I50.000.--
           I7 √ Modèle 74 - Robe de chenille noire...........  200.000.--
            √ Modèle 95 - Manteau de lainage noir..........  I60.000.--
            √ Modèle 44 - Manteau de lainage pied de poule
                 noir et blanc..............................  I60.000.--
           24 √ Modèle 33 - Robe d'organza violet...........  I40.000.--
            √ Pelisse de lainage noir avec fourrage d'her-
                 mine noire à Madame........................  I60.000.--
            √ Pelisse de lainage natté gris, doublé de
                 castor à Madame............................  I60.000.--
Réglé par Chèque
Nº 1287 Date
Sur                                                          4.660.000.--
   BALENCIAGA, S.A.        Déduction des Taxes..............    652.400.--

            SOIT : II.483 DOLLARS                            4.007.600.--
                       39.2
            =======================================
                 II,875
```

A shopping trip in Paris in November 1956 for Mona Williams included a stop at Balenciaga. This bill totaling $11,875 was most likely one of many on that trip. Williams was married to Count Bismarck at the time of this shopping trip.

Mona appears with Cecil Beaton, famed fashion and portrait photographer. They remained friends for many years.

Standing in front of the stable on the Harrison Williams estate are Walton and Arthur Davis. The tower in the background was the water supply for the estate.

A generous gift was made to the village in 1954 when Mona Williams gave 27 acres of land to Bayville. Her only restriction was that the land stayed undeveloped and natural. The current sign at the entrance to the woods is in her husband's name. The village has maintained and preserved the Harrison Williams Woods ever since.

A. Winslow Valentine, Bayville's postmaster, became mayor in the post–World War II years from 1948 to 1953. It was during this time that part of the Harrison Williams estate was gifted to the village. It included the complex that houses the village hall, museum, library, and what is now Harrison Williams Woods. Valentine was instrumental in the planning and construction of the village war memorials.

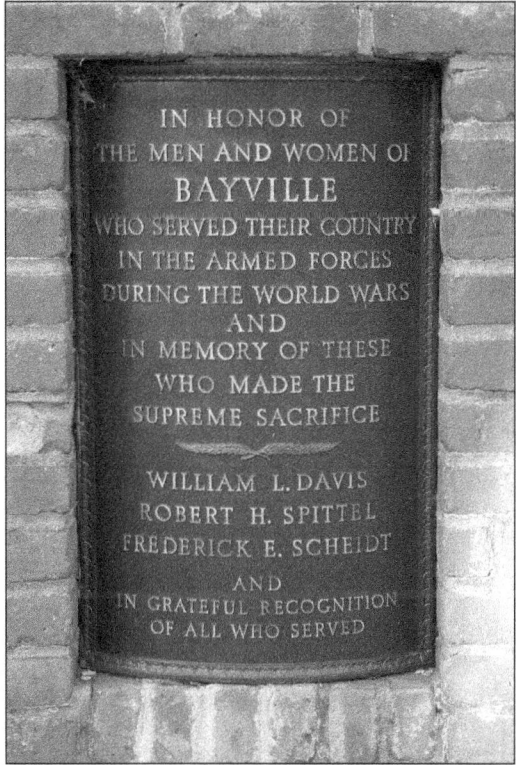

War memorials for World War I, World War II, the Korean War, and the Vietnam conflict were erected on the village green at the village hall complex. These monuments are dedicated to the memory of the men and women who served their country and stand as a reminder to all residents of the sacrifice made by these brave individuals. Each year on Memorial Day, all veterans are remembered at a ceremony and wreaths are placed by the monuments to honor them.

Edward F. Brickell served as mayor from 1953 until 1962. He was helpful in acquiring both Creek Road and West Harbor Road beach properties for the village. During his tenure, Mona Williams, who was then known as Countess Von Bismarck, fought to downsize the zoning of property lots of the estate of her late husband Harrison Williams to lots of a smaller size than proposed by the village. As a result, Bayville's zoning laws changed.

One of New York's leading architects, designers, and decorators, Edward Knuriem built this Victorian summer residence in 1895. The building sat on six acres and had commanding views of Long Island Sound and Connecticut. Fronting on Bayville Avenue, the carriage house and servants quarters were across the street. In 1943, the building was sold to the William Indianos family, and it became the Bayville Hotel. It was torn down in 1963.

In 1906, the Callender house was built by Peter Winchester Rouss. It was the Rouss family summer home until it was sold in 1932 to Robert Livingston Clarkson, a prominent civic leader. In 1961, it was opened as the Oyster Bay Hospital in Bayville. Sold again in 1970, the Callender house was renamed the Renaissance. In 1984, it became the home to the Cerebral Palsy Association of Nassau County. The 10-acre estate is located between Merritt Lane and Beaver Drive, fronting on Bayville Avenue.

As it stood facing the Long Island Sound, the Rouss mansion had panoramic views across to Connecticut. Many balls and huge parties were held in the 65-room mansion. Stone steps, magnificently manicured gardens, and a rolling lawn made for a beautiful walk down to the beach.

The beautiful interior of the Rouss estate reflected the opulence of the era. The rooms were adorned with exquisite furnishings and artwork. Chandeliers, gilded mirrors, and carved molding enhanced the magnificent decor. Reception rooms and bedrooms alike were furnished with the finest antiques, tapestries, rugs, and luxurious fabrics. Although it was only the family's summer home, the estate was elaborately decorated. It was common practice that the summer home be as elegant as the year-round residence.

View along the Shore, Showing H. Rainsforth's Residence, Bayville, L. I.

The Rainsforth residence once sat on the bluff looking out over Long Island Sound west of Merritt Lane. After sitting vacant for many years, the property was sold, and the estate was torn down to make way for the construction of new homes on what are now Donald Street, Leeward Cove, and Willow Street (the Sound Side Estates).

The Nunnakoma Park-on-the-Sound residence, when offered for sale, was advertised as a modern residence that was fireproof and was situated on two and one half acres of waterfront property at what are now Quannacut and Wayaawi Avenues. The mansion's amenities included a large reception room, a ballroom, a conservatory with a pool, and a 100-foot-long, glass-covered, open porch.

The back porch of the Nunnakoma Park-on-the-Sound overlooked the expansive, beautifully landscaped grounds that contained a large variety of trees and shrubs and a fabulous view of the waterfront. The wide, spacious lawns ran down to meet the sandy beach.

Three

BRIDGES AND FERRIES

The first bridge linking Bayville to Mill Neck was constructed of wood and only lasted until 1904. The original cost to construct the bridge was $5,000. The second bridge, built in 1906, was financed by the Town of Oyster Bay and utilized modern steel truss construction. Problems arose with the second bridge due to the horse-and-carriage traffic. The wooden roadway on the bridge was laid horizontally, causing the carriage wheels and hoofs of the horses to gouge ruts in the roadway.

This is West Shore Road in 1898, looking north from Oyster Bay to Bayville. In that same year, a wooden bridge at the end of the road connected the two communities.

Many improvements to the road can be seen in this 1920 view of West Shore Road. Properties have been landscaped, telephone poles can be seen, and the road has been widened and improved to accommodate the increased traffic.

Construction of the third Bayville bridge began in 1922 and lasted for several months. Crews worked on a tight schedule, and automobile traffic was diverted through Locust Valley and Mill Neck, while pedestrians had the option of taking a water taxi across Oyster Bay Harbor.

With much fanfare, the third bridge opened in 1922. It was estimated that over 1,000 people participated in the day's events. The opening ceremonies included a parade with floats and fire departments from all the neighboring communities. Mayor A. Winslow Pierce and other county officials gave speeches. Town of Oyster Bay supervisor Chester Painter dedicated the structure.

A huge turnout of Bayville residents and visitors from the surrounding communities came to the opening-day ceremony for the new bridge.

In 1938, the construction of the fourth bridge was completed. The old bridge was dynamited and removed by crane. There were hopes that the footing of the old bridge could be reused, but an inspection found them to be unacceptable. This new drawbridge was electronically operated. When the third bridge was opened, many residents believed it would be the last. However, 17 years later, residents saw construction of the fourth bridge.

An aerial view shows the bridge in the late 1960s looking north toward Bayville, with the Mill Neck Creek on the left and Oyster Bay Harbor on the right.

The clean lines and classic structure of the Bayville bridge are a beautiful sight in the early morning hours on this clear day.

An early attraction in Bayville was a tour along the waters of Mill Neck Creek or just a lazy day spent fishing.

Seen boating in Mill Neck Creek in the early 1900s from left to right are D. D. Smith, Mabel Snedecker, Eva Hendrickson, and ? Bedell. Behind the motor launch *Vanessa* is the second Bayville drawbridge. In the background is the shoreline of Mill Neck Creek.

A number of ferries line up at the dock by Sound Beach Avenue ready to transport passengers and automobiles to Stamford, Rye, and Manhattan.

Located on the sound side of Bayville Avenue near the present-day Crescent Beach Club, the ferry *Sankaty* made its last voyage to Connecticut in the fall of 1937 from Ferry Beach.

An invaluable form of transportation for many travelers, the Bayville ferry is at the dock awaiting passengers for its journey to Rye.

The old meets new, as seen in the early photograph of a sound-side beach. Cars, horses, and buggies are parked along the beach while their occupants enjoy the sun and the sand.

Four

WATERFRONT

The rumrunner *William T. Bell* had the same name as one of Bayville's founding fathers. In a February 1927 storm, a northeast wind caused the boat to run aground on Oak Point. The crew came ashore and quickly disappeared. As word spread of the boat's cargo of illegal liquor, it disappeared even quicker. Local residents did not notify the authorities until a day and a half later.

After all the cargo and liquor disappeared from the ship, the *William T. Bell* needed to be removed from the beach. After several unsuccessful attempts by the U.S. Coast Guard to tow the ship from the beach, it was decided that explosives would be the best way to remove the wreck. The explosives were set, and the *Bell* was blasted. The demolition of the *William T. Bell* proved to be a difficult task. The *Bell* was a tough, old ship; the blast only destroyed the decking and the wheelhouse, while the hull remained intact. It took many hours of hard, manual labor to remove the boat piece by piece from the beach.

The program printed for Pres. Theodore Roosevelt's review of the U.S. Atlantic Fleet contained the names and lineup of the ships as they appeared for inspection by the president and dignitaries aboard his yacht off the shores of Bayville in September 1906.

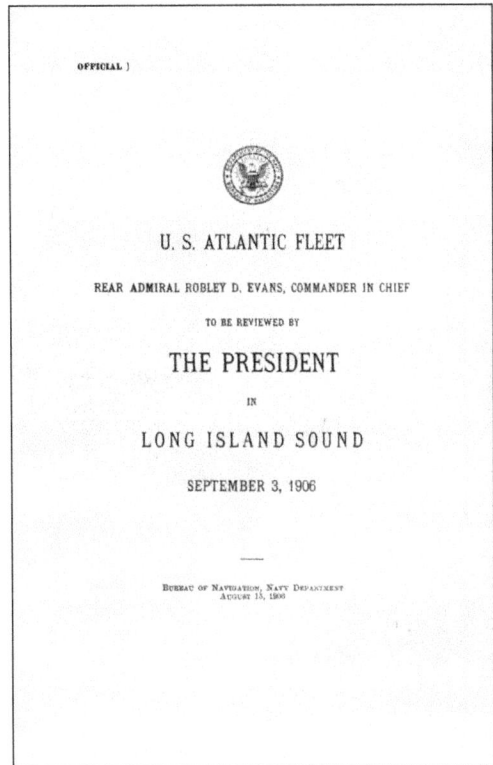

U. S. ATLANTIC FLEET

REAR ADMIRAL ROBLEY D. EVANS, COMMANDER IN CHIEF

TO BE REVIEWED BY

THE PRESIDENT

IN

LONG ISLAND SOUND

SEPTEMBER 3, 1906

Bureau of Navigation, Navy Department
August 15, 1906

During the Russo-Japanese War in 1906, the U.S. Atlantic Fleet was summoned by Roosevelt for a naval review. The presidential yacht the *Mayflower* traveled out of Oyster Bay Harbor with the Russian and Japanese delegations aboard to review the flotilla of 40 military ships. This event was an important factor in leading to the end of the war. As a result of his efforts to bring an end to the war, Roosevelt was awarded the Nobel Peace Prize in 1906—the first American to receive this honor.

Wall's Wharf remains as popular today as it was in 1945 when it was called Wall's Beach, a great place for refreshments and of course the beach. Today's patrons can see the history of Wall's in the display of photographs that are part of the restaurant's decor.

Renting a rowboat at Wall's Beach was a favorite pastime. It provided an opportunity to row for pleasure or get out on Long Island Sound for a day of fishing.

It has long been rumored that there was a submarine sunk in the shallow waters off Wall's Beach. In fact, there were actually up to four World War I submarines. The operators of the ferry company had them scuttled off Wall's Beach around 1922 as a breakwater in an attempt to protect the ferry pier. Navy records cannot verify the exact identity of the submarines, as the vessels' records end with their sale as scrap in 1922, and no records can be found of the sale from any of the scrap yards to the ferry company.

On Center Island Beach at the east end of Bayville, workers set up camps. Each morning, the foreman walked through the camps to hire laborers to build and work on the neighboring Centre Island estates.

Over time, the laborers' tent camp was replaced by summer bungalows. These bungalows were torn down in the 1940s.

The town of Oyster Bay owned the beachfront property and bathhouse at what is now Centre Island Beach. A tunnel under the road allows access to Oyster Bay Harbor and Long Island Sound. The homes pictured on the beach were demolished when the 99-year lease held on the property by the village expired in 1968.

In the early 1900s, residents gathered at the Valentine boathouse and Valentine Beach on Mill Neck Creek for a day of boating, swimming, and fishing. On a hot summer day, Valentine Beach was a popular place enjoyed by many.

The small cabins in the background are former barracks moved from Camp Mills in Garden City after World War I to this location at Winslow Wilson Beach where these young children are enjoying a day in the water. In later years, the cabins were replaced by new homes.

By the 1920s, it became obvious that Oak Neck needed a bathing pavilion. Located right at the beach, the pavilion was a welcome addition to the beachfront, which accommodated all the visitors who came to Bayville to enjoy the sun and the surf. Upstairs porches at the Oak Neck Beach House provided a pleasant place to sit and enjoy the breeze and wonderful views of Long Island Sound.

The waters surrounding Bayville have been important not only for industry but also for recreation. The Bayville Aquatic Club started as a swimming club in 1923. The club, which later became known as the Bayville Yacht Club, leased a building in Oyster Bay Harbor at what is now West Harbor Beach. The club expanded its activities to include outboard motorboating. The club's swim team won national championships for both boys and girls. The outboard racing team was at one time the largest in the East. The membership dropped drastically in 1932, and the club was forced to close due to lack of funds.

In September 1938, a powerful hurricane made landfall on the south shore of Long Island. High winds and driving rain caused tremendous devastation as the storm raced north across the island and on to Connecticut. The storm surge caused major flooding in Bayville, and the bay met the sound. The "Long Island Express," as it was sometimes referred, demolished many homes and establishments. The Oak Neck bathhouse was one of many casualties.

In 1954, floodwaters filled the property of the Texaco station located on the corner of Ludlam and First Avenues. Pictured by the pumps are June Heimrich Burke (left) and Dorothy Jones Sordi.

The only form of transportation that was available after a storm that left the streets of Bayville flooded was a rowboat. Harry Minicozzi and Dorothy Jones Sordi are seen rowing their boat through the parking lot of the Texaco station.

Five

COMMUNITY SERVICES

Nicholas Godfrey, who was the postmaster at the time, donated the land to build this two-room schoolhouse in 1895. A two-room addition was added in 1910. The building was located on Schoolhouse Road, now known as School Street. By 1920, the number of students had grown, requiring the district to rent space in the basement of the village church.

Until Bayville's first schoolhouse was constructed, students attended school in Oyster Bay. Since the bridge had yet to be constructed connecting Bayville and Oyster Bay, students had to travel through Locust Valley, Mill Neck, past Beaver Dam, down Cleft Road to West Shore Road, and into Oyster Bay, while others rowed across Mill Neck Creek. On what is now Merritt Lane, Amos Merritt donated property for this one-room schoolhouse of board and batten construction. The first teacher, Aaron Payne, taught all the 34 students in grades one through eight.

The school board of trustees used this contract to hire teacher Alice Andrews in 1902. The term of her employment was 32 consecutive weeks at a monthly compensation of $50. Her classroom was in the two-room schoolhouse on School Street.

Souvenir

Bayville Union School

Primary Department

DISTRICT NO. 6.

Oyster Bay Township,
Nassau County, N. Y.

Term 1903-1904.

COMPLIMENTS OF

C. ELVIRA BROWN,

TEACHER.

Motto: "Never give up"

Pupils.

Louise Beatty	Helen Beatty
George Beatty	Loretta Bell
Addie Cheshire	Howard Cheshire
John Colgan	Ethel Corson
Vincenzo Ceraso	Angelo Ceraso
Arthur Davis	George Dorber
Edna Dorber	Wallace Downs
Madeline Di Fede	Antoinette Di Fede
Mary Di Fede	Madeline Ellison
Harold Ellison	Dora Finnin
Cora E. Flower	Lizzie Fusaro
Dolores Fusaro	R. Stuart Frazer
William H. Hahn	Henry Hahn
Irwin S. Hendrickson	Albert S. Howell
Alice Jensen	Agnes Jensen
Harry Lockwood	Arthur Lockwood
John McCaffrey	Stephen Rosell
Mamie Ringle	De Etta Pillois
Blanche Sackett	Mildred Sackett
Alma Schenck	Lucy Temple
Arthur Temple	Wilber R. Tilford
Evelyn M. Tilford	Mary L. Tilford
Blanche Wansor	Claudius Wansor

The Bayville Union School District No. 6 Primary Department had an enrollment of 46 students for the 1903–1904 term. Teacher C. Elvira Brown created this souvenir roster for the students. "Never give up" was the motto. Many descendants of these students still live in the village today.

Children pose for a picture in front of the two-room schoolhouse where classes for several grades were held in the same room. As was common in those times, teachers had the challenging task of teaching children in several different grades in one classroom.

Located on a path in the woods behind the second school was a huge rock that was referred to as "Indian Rock" by the schoolchildren. This was their meeting place on the way to and from school. One morning, a large, white cross appeared that had not been there the night before. For many years, the white cross reappeared as bright as ever as soon as it began to fade. The rock became known as "Spooky Rock."

In 1932, David Delano Clark divulged the secret of Spooky Rock while on his deathbed. Clark was a school janitor who was painting the building and one day decided to clean his brush by wiping it against the rock. When news spread of the appearance of a cross on the rock, he decided to keep it a secret. Each year, as it began to fade, he repainted it, keeping it a secret and perpetuating the legend.

By the 1920s, the little schoolhouse with the two-room addition was the home to high school as well as the elementary grades. On this sunny day, headmaster Arthur B. Monroe is seen sitting in front of the schoolhouse with, from left to right, Mildred Van Allen, Emma Bush, Arabella Jamison, and Helen Williams.

By the early 1930s, the number of school-age children had grown to 150. The little schoolhouse and auxiliary locations in the church basement could no longer accommodate all the children attending the Bayville School. Plans were drawn up to build a new school on Mountain Avenue. With construction underway, villagers attended the dedication ceremony of the third school.

The property for Bayville's third school was purchased from Fred King and Albert Sielke. The Colonial-style structure opened in 1931. This was the new quarters for 150 children. With keen foresight, the building was designed so that additions could be readily made. In 1959, Bayville became part of Central School District No. 3, now known as the Locust Valley Central School District, which includes Bayville, Brookville, and Locust Valley. The first addition to the school was built in 1961.

Here is one of the first classes in the new, third school in 1933. From left to right are (first row) Cleo Tweedy, Joan Holms, Curtis Wall, Vincent Flanagan, Margaret Abeel, Mary Sanzoverino, and Marie Tappen; (second row) Doris Johnson, Lillian Hall, Harrison Mackey, Chick Ferraco, Eugene Hill, John Strigaro, Jack Van Sise, Mildred Cunningham, and Kathline Abeel.

The students of the graduating class of 1934 from left to right are (first row) Joan Holm, Doris Johnson, Mary Ann McCoun, unidentified, Cleo Tweedy, Kathline Abeel, Saphire Hawhurst, and unidentified; (second row) Lillian Hall, Verna Sheahy, ? Davis (teacher), Mildred Cunningham, and Harrison Mackey; (third row) Chick Ferraco, Eugene Flanagan, Curtis Wall, Reginald Benton, Eugene Hill, and Jack Van Sise.

Miss Schmidt's class is pictured in 1940. From left to right are (first row) Marie Cozzeto, Florence Taylor, Patty Trainor, Jane Martineau, Archie Strigaro, unidentified, Billy Martin, Robert Valentine, and Jerry Roslund; (second row) Ruth Sanzoverino, Josie Baird, unidentified, unidentified, Robert Davis, Charles Sterling, George Blackman, and unidentified; (third row) Margaret Faust, Freddie Ammirata, George Granger, Joan Ellison, and Patricia Seaman; (fourth row) Schmidt.

The Bayville School band practices for a concert on the porch of what is now the Bayville Intermediate School.

On the first and last days of school, from the two-room schoolhouse to the new school on Mountain Avenue, the bell was rung. In 1945, the bell was dedicated to Albert W. Flower, who served for many years on the board of education.

As the population in Bayville grew, so did the need for more classrooms. Bayville Primary School was built in 1962 to accommodate the growing student population.

In 1976, a time capsule was buried on the grounds of the village hall complex to commemorate the 200th anniversary of the United States.

Nicholas Godfrey was appointed as the first postmaster in 1877 by Pres. Grover Cleveland. The post office at that time was located in the Dickerson home. Mail was delivered by postal riders from Locust Valley to the Dickerson home where residents then stopped by to collect their letters. The Finnin Hall building pictured here became the first official post office in 1910, but home delivery was not established until 1961.

In 1915, Bayville Avenue was called Main Street. Looking east at Merritt Lane, this view shows St. Paul's United Methodist Church of Bayville (known as the Village Church) on the left and the post office building on the right.

With a bequest from Ester J. Valentine in 1859, land was purchased for $150 for the construction of a six-room parsonage. In 1902, the Village Church, as it was known, became St. Paul's United Methodist Church. In 1960, when a new church was constructed on Mountain Avenue, the building was sold to Wallace Leitner. It housed his interior decorating business. Today it is a privately owned residence.

APPROVED PLANS for NEW VILLAGE CHURCH

(Adapted from the Architect's preliminary drawings, with latest revisions)

1959

Note: To simplify this sketch we have omitted location of the windows, but they can be seen in the artist's sketch.

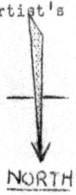

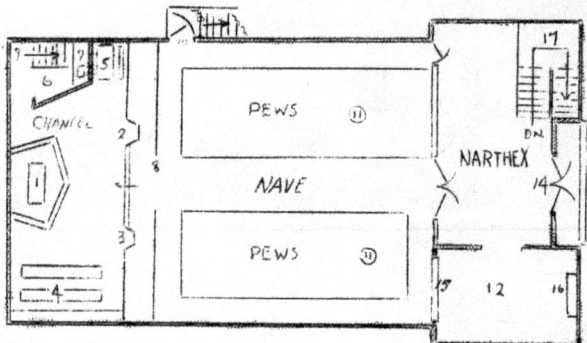

NORTH

MAIN FLOOR PLAN

LEGEND

1. Holy Table
2. Pulpit
3. Lectern
4. Choir Pews
5. Organ Console
6. Sacristy

7. Flower sink
8. Communion Rail
9. Stairs to lower floor
10. Fire Exit
11. Pews, seating 185 persons

12. Chapel and sound-proof "Cry-room"
14. Mountain Avenue Entrance
15. Window
16. Worship Center
17. Stairs to lower floor

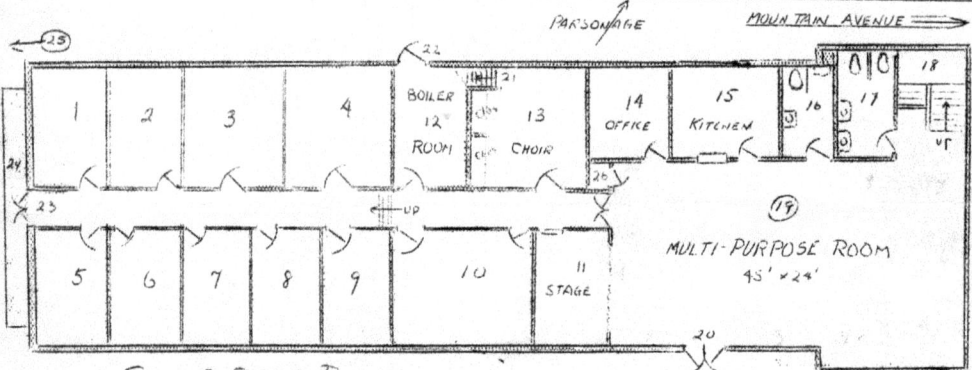

GROUND FLOOR PLAN

LEGEND

1,2,5,6,7,8,9:
  9 x 15' classrooms
3,4: - 13 x 15' classrooms
10: - 15 x 18' classroom
11: - 9 x 15' stage-classroom
12: - Boiler Room
13: - 15 x 15' Choir & class room
14: - 10 x 11' Office-classroom

15. Kitchen
16. Men's Lavatory
17. Powder Room
18. Stairway to Narthex and Mountain Avenue
19. Multi-purpose room 45 x 24'
20. Door to Driveway

21. Sacristy Stairs
22. Boiler Room Exit
23. Door to Parking Area
24. Rain Shelter
25. Parking Area
26. Closet

Plans were drawn up for a new village church after the old church, which had undergone many structural changes over the years, became too small. Plans included a larger church on the main floor and a kitchen, several classrooms, restrooms, a multipurpose room, and offices in the basement.

An acre and a half that was bequeathed to the church in Harrison Williams's will became the site for the new village church. Construction began on it in the late 1950s. The new church was bigger and had more rooms than the old church to meet the needs of the growing congregation. The parsonage was built in 1956, and the church was completed in 1960.

When the first chapel was built in 1909, St. Gertrude's was a mission church under the administration of St. Dominic's Parish of Oyster Bay. The building was enlarged in 1937 and was established as a separate parish in 1959. Located on the corner of Bayville Avenue and School Street, the church had its 100-year jubilee celebration in June 2009.

Over the years, St. Gertrude's Church has had several renovations. Changes to the original structure included moving the steeple and adding an expansion to the back of the church. In April 1978, St. Gertrude's Parish Center opened. Fr. Thomas Connolly was pastor when the building was constructed. Today St. Gertrude's Parish Center is home to a preschool, used for religious education classes, CYO basketball, and many church and community meetings and functions.

The official seal for the incorporated village of Bayville is a portrait of a Native American, representing the original inhabitants of the area.

Bayville Village Hall, located on School Street, was part of the stable complex on the Harrison Williams estate.

The Bayville Historical Museum was founded by Gladys Mack in 1972. Located in the village hall complex, the building was at one time the chauffeur's residence for the Pierce estate and later the Harrison Williams estate.

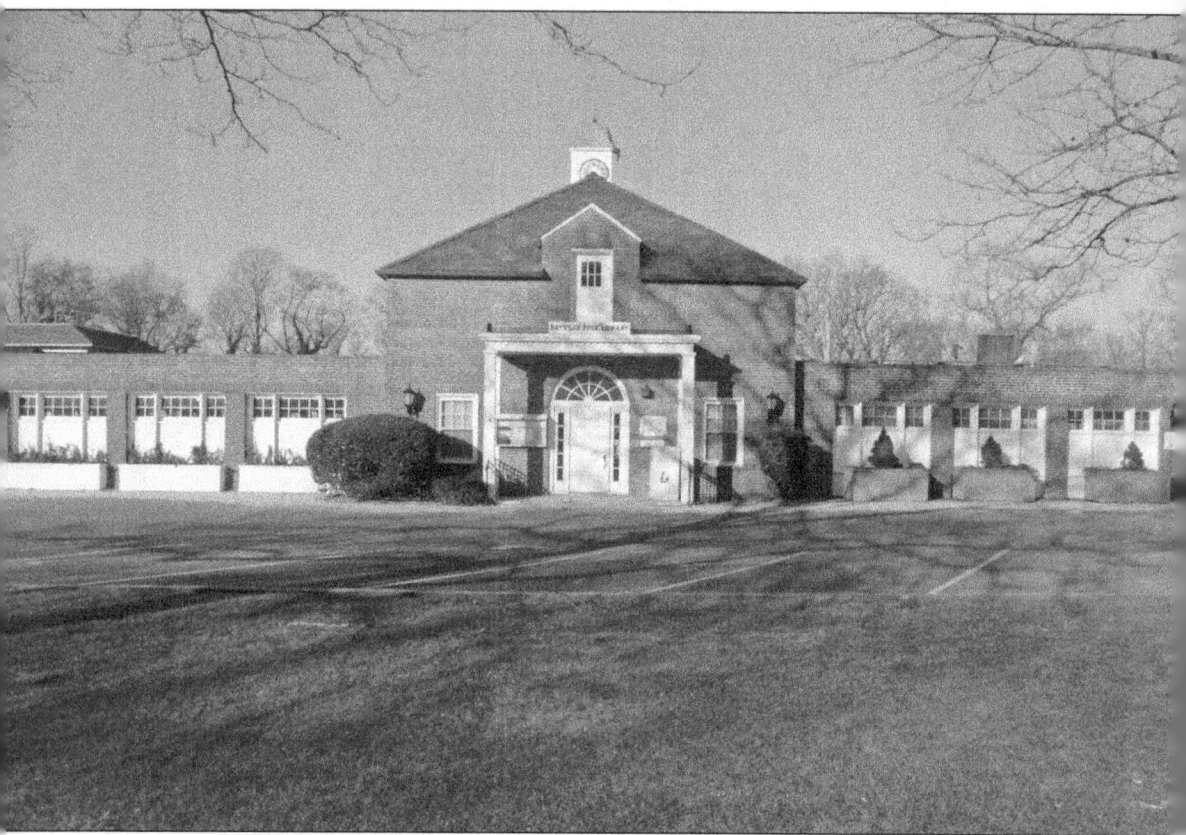

The origin of the library goes back to 1903. In a small store on Merritt Lane, Josephine Cortelyou allowed her sickly 12-year-old grandson Albert DeLoach to rent his books to any customers who were interested. He started with 12 books until several local women decided to raise money and collect books for him. Over the next several years, the library moved numerous times, first to the second floor of the Finnin Hall building and next to what is now Library Lane. In May 1912, the library received its charter from the Regents University of the State of New York. In 1956, it became part of the village hall complex in the space that was originally the stables for the Harrison Williams estate.

Men trained to be motorcycle officers at the New York State School for Police in Troy. The department grew from two to five officers in the 1920s. Prior to that time, police protection came from a town constable and state troopers. These officers from left to right are John Casey, Steve Rosell, Wilbur Tilford, ? Wernerbach, and George Cook.

Over the years, the Bayville Police Department changed from motorcycles to patrol cars. Pictured in 1953, these officers from left to right are Sandy Belsito, Mel Placilla, Harry Porteus, Bob Klipera, and Sam Coruzzi. The police station was located at the village hall complex. The Bayville Police Department was in existence until 1962, when it was replaced by the Nassau County Police Department.

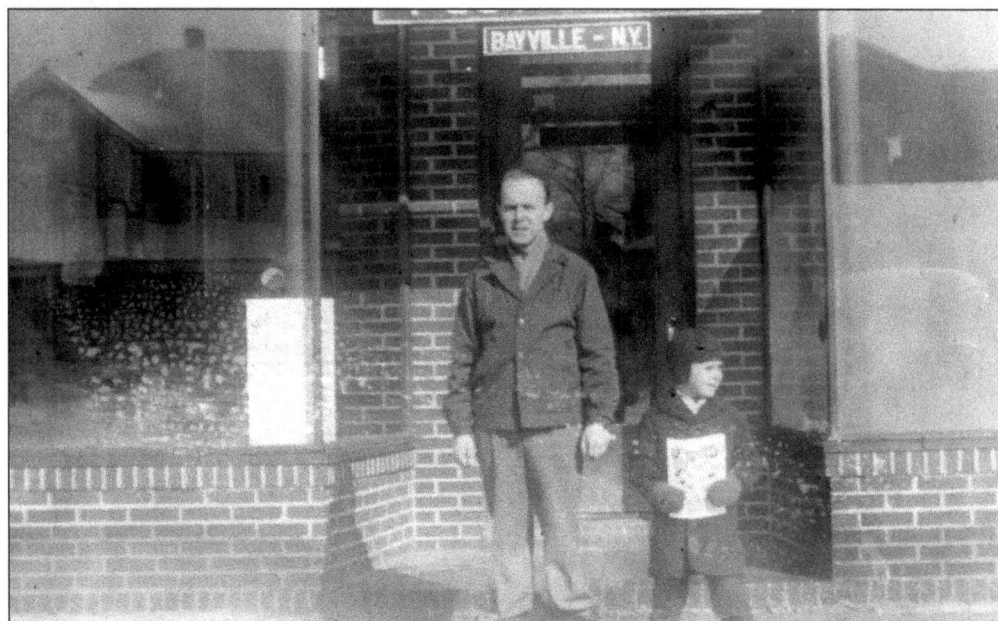

The Bayville Post Office moved many times since it was first established in 1877. Here in front of the Bayville Avenue location around 1946 are Quentin E. Schoverling (left) and R. W. Schoverling III.

Erected in 1923, the Bayville Fire Company's first firehouse was a 24-foot structure. The building was constructed on land owned by Elizabeth Godfrey. The growth of the village and the long response time for firefighters and their equipment to arrive from neighboring villages prompted the community to realize the need for its own fire company.

At a cost of $7,500, the Bayville Fire Company purchased it first pumper in 1923. The pumper, an American LaFrance, had the capacity to carry 400 gallons and was a much-needed piece of equipment for the Bayville firemen. The manufacturer of the truck was a company founded by Truckson LaFrance. Still in business today, the company is the premier manufacturer of firefighting equipment.

Pictured in front of the firehouse, the 1925 tournament team from left to right includes (first row) Ted Mackey, ? Davis, and LeRoy Seaman; (second row) Louis Valentine, Arthur Davis, ? Martinaeu, Henry McCaffrey, James Frontero, George Cook, and Ed Ellison.

From the first pumper to additional pumpers and a ladder truck, the Bayville Fire Company continued to keep up with the growing number of residents. Its state-of-the-art equipment and volunteer firemen greatly serve the community.

Bayville, with its growing population, was in need of a larger firehouse and more equipment. A building committee was formed that included Henry McCaffery (chairman), Peter Pennington, Martin McCaffery, Louis Valentine, George Jensen, Theodore Mackey, and John Roulette as committee members. Plans were drawn, and the new building was completed in 1929 at a cost of $60,000.

With the installation of a new alarm system and the purchase of new equipment, Bayville had a fire department to rival neighboring communities. The Bayville Fire Company not only protects Bayville but also the village of Centre Island and parts of the village of Mill Neck.

Six

LEISURE

The lineup of 1909 players from left to right includes (first row) Eina Jensen, Harry Anderson, Otis West, George Jensen, Martin McCaffrey, and Rink O'Reilly; (second row) Edward Tilford, John Dean, Len Wansor, Louis Valentine, Peter Cocks (umpire), Dan Ellison Sr., and George Hall.

A busy summer day at Creek Beach included swimming, boating, and diving. Today Creek Beach is home to boat slips for village residents, and it is a popular fishing spot.

"Bayville Beauties" pose for a special feature written for the *New York Times*. The article hoped to promote Bayville and entice more people to visit.

The stands behind the Bayville Casino were often filled with many fans enjoying America's favorite pastime. The baseball field was located on the property behind the casino—a great, flat piece of property with ample parking. The only drawback was that at this location there were times when a game could be called because of high tide. When the outfield was underwater, the game had to end.

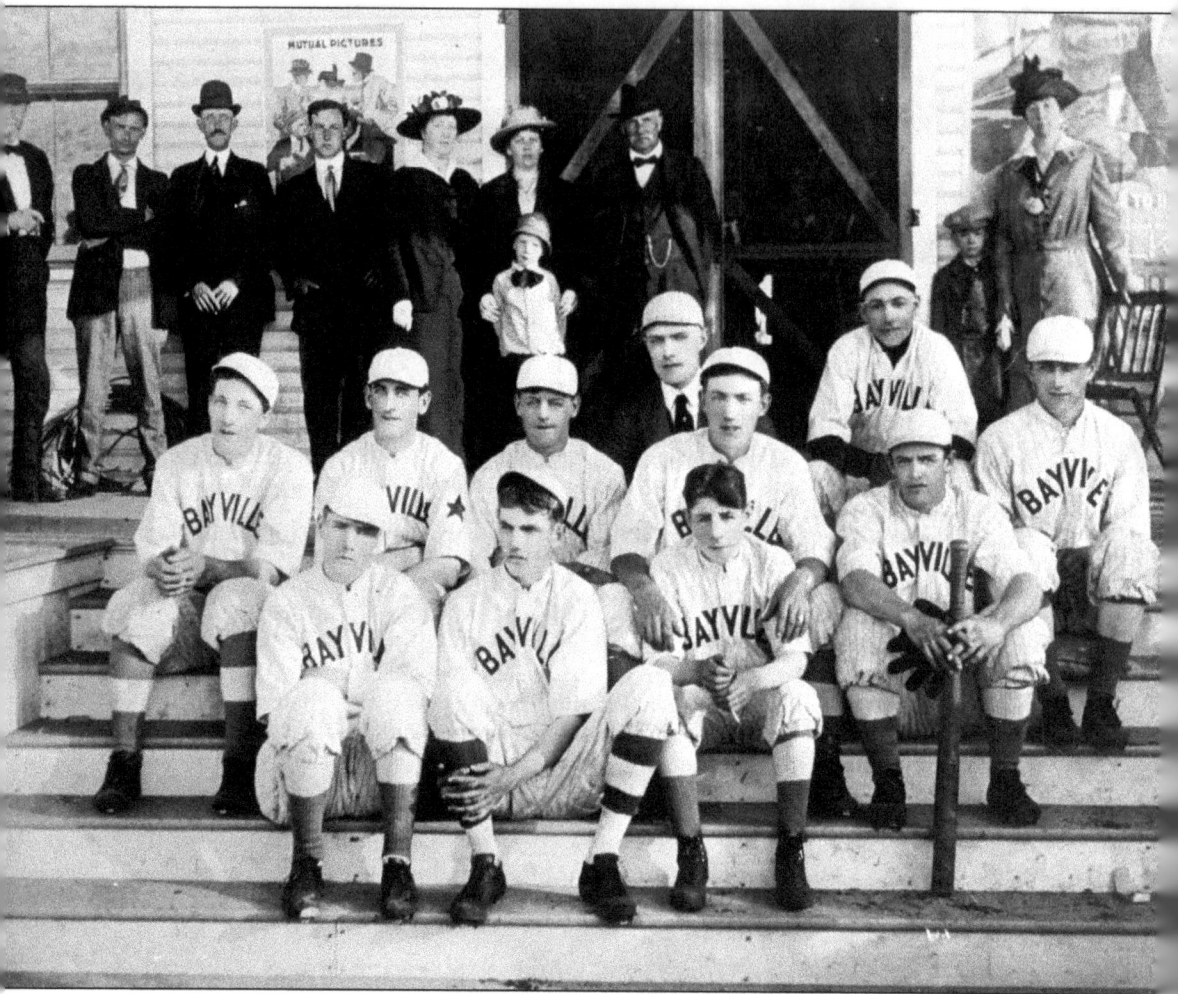

On the steps of the Bayville Casino from left to right are (first row) Irwin Hendrickson, Sam Taylor, and Wesley Raymus; (second row) Claude Wansor, Martin McCaffery, Steve Roselle, George Jensen, Jack McCaffery, and unidentified; (third row) Howard Taylor and unidentified. Standing in the background are William Dean, Bob Denhan, Sam Taylor Sr., unidentified, Elsie Tilford, Hattie Tilford and brother Billy Stevens, Lottie Tilford, Robert Tilford, and Zeb Wilson Jr.

Young and old alike joined together to share their love of the game. The 1915 baseball team from left to right includes (first row) George Jensen, Irwin Hendrickson, and Leonard Davis; (second row) ? Griffen, George Darber, John Donovan, and Sam Taylor; (third row) Edgar Wright, Dave Ellison, Howard Taylor, Martin McCaffery, and Walton Davis.

FOOTBALL GAME SPONSORED BY
L. V. FIRE DEP'T

Sunday, December 6, 1931

L. V. YELLOW JACKETS
VS.

87   BAYVILLE A. A.

School Field, Locust Valley, N. Y.

KICK OFF 2 P. M.   RAIN OR SHINE
Admission 50c (Right to Refund Admission Reserved).

The Locust Valley Fire Department sponsored this football game that featured Bayville versus Locust Valley on a Sunday afternoon. The game provided an afternoon of entertainment for the firemen, their families, and football fans from both communities.

The 1946 America Legion baseball team from left to right includes (first row) Ike Ferraco, Jack McLean, Joe Ferraco, bat boy Billy Reilly, James Guido, Donald Placilla, and John Mazure; (second row) Albert Taylor, unidentified, Ralph Abraham, Anthony "Chick" Ferraco, manager Joe Schmidt, Eddie Watson, Mickey Ammirata, and Dominick Cullire.

Long before there were playgrounds with swings, seesaws, and monkey bars, a hayloft was a great place to play. Many an afternoon was spent in the hayloft. Pictured here is Paul Davis.

Even the family dog braved the cold and joined these adventurous men for an afternoon on the ice at Mill Neck Creek. From left to right are George Jensen, Joe Davis, and Louis Valentine.

The Arlington

is known as one of the best and foremost Hotels on the North shore of Long Island; 250 feet above sea level, facing Long Island Sound in the north and Oyster Bay Harbor in the south and east. Across the Sound Stamford, Conn. meets the eye. It is known as the coolest and prettiest spot on L. I.; no mosquitoes, always cool and breezy. This Hotel is located only about 300 feet from L. I. Sound and on one of the finest Automobile Roads known as the Shore Road of Long Island and only 10 minutes ride by auto from Oyster Bay R. R. Station. A large veranda of about 1,600 square feet gives accommodation and a grand view of the surroundings. The Hotel is patronized only by the best kind of people. Our cuisine is unexcelled, the kitchen is in charge of a first-class Vienna chef and under the direct supervision of the wife of the proprietor.

The Arlington Hotel brochure described the location and amenities it offered. Notice that the hotel had a special room rate for maids who often traveled with the family for whom they worked. All the amenities of a top-class hotel were offered at the Arlington. The hotel invited interested patrons to inspect the premises and assured them that they would be pleased with all that the hotel had to offer its guests.

Automobiles for pleasure parties can be obtained at very low rates at the Hotel.

Theatre and Moving Picture Shows are only 10 minutes ride by Auto from the Hotel at Oyster Bay.

The proprietor arranges dances, parties and all kinds of Amusements for the benefit of the guests.

An up-to-date Cafe and Grill Room furnished with a first-class Billiard and Pool Table for the convenience of those who wish to patronize the same.

The service is first-class and the help polite and experienced.

We serve A la Carte or Table d'Hote.

Communication for commuters is very low.

Terms: $2.50 and up per day, $15.00 and up per week according to the location of rooms.

Special rates for children and maids.

We extend to you our heartiest invitation for inspection and assure you that you will be more than pleased after you have seen this place and will not hesitate to make your reservation in due time. Hoping to have the pleasure to greet you.

Very truly yours

G. PICK, Proprietor

The popularity of Bayville grew, and so did the Arlington Hotel, which was located on the south side of Bayville Avenue near East Slope Road. Guests had a choice of rooms with water views of the Long Island Sound or southern views of Oyster Bay Harbor. In later years, the Arlington Hotel became Camp Sunshine. The camp provided a summer residence for young women who worked in New York City. Summers in Bayville were a welcome change from the hot city.

In 1913, the Bayville Casino was known by residents and visitors alike as the place for entertainment. On the ground floor was a restaurant, and on the second floor was a dance hall that doubled as a movie theater. The basement contained a roller-skating rink. The casino was destroyed by a fire in 1924. Years later, the Pig 'N Whistle, a popular dining establishment, was built on the same site.

Enjoying the sunny afternoon, this member of the class of 1928 is sitting in a favorite spot outside the store on Friendly Corner. What a great place to see all the comings and goings of the village as he reads his newspaper.

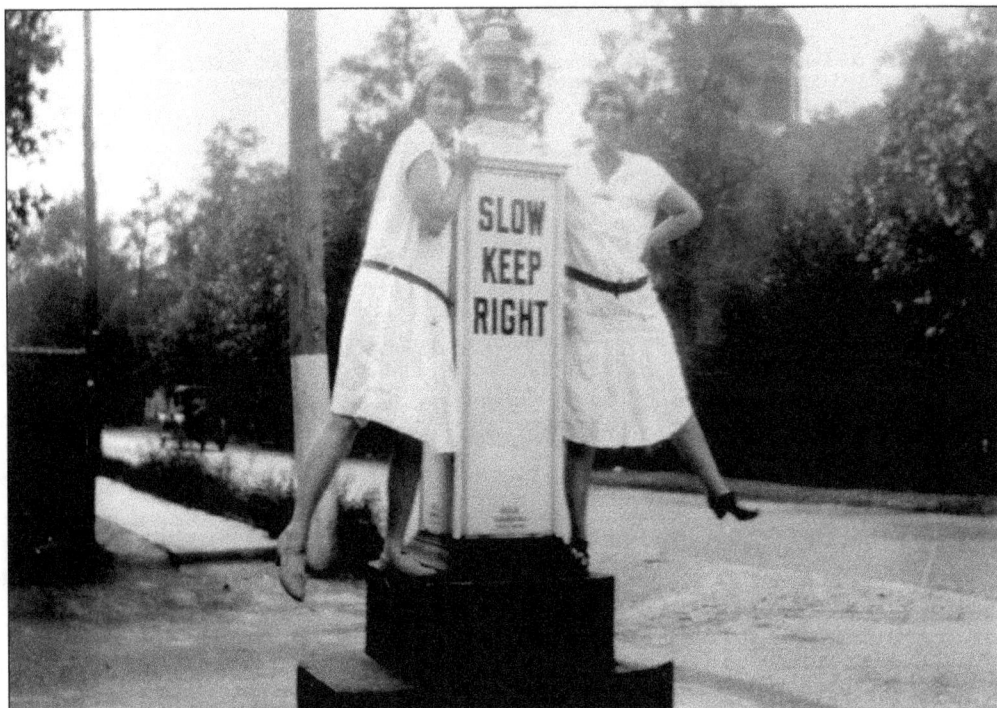

At Friendly Corner in 1930, Sadie and Louise Tilford strike a pose and share some laughs at the traffic warning light located at the corner of Perry and Bayville Avenues.

Bobsled team Bayville 1911 set a record in 1920 when the sled passed the half-mile marker with a time of 37.4 seconds at 60 miles per hour. Team members from left to right are Martin McCaffery, Arthur Davis, Herman Spittel, Wesley Raymus, Patrick Trainor, Irving Hendrickson, Harold Ellison, Louis West, Arvine Tillotson, Joe Davis, Walter Dudley, Ray Gildersleve, Harvey Smith, George Darber, George Jensen, Labbie Wansor, Charles DeForest, Paul Davis, Edgar Wright, and Ed Tilford. The bobsled was built by Henry Dunzion of Locust Valley and sold to Zeb Wilson of Bayville. It is on exhibit at the Long Island Museum in Stonybrook.

This bobsled team was an all-women-and-one-man team. They completed the mile in 42 seconds at the annual bobsled meet in Huntington, Long Island. At the time, bobsledding was a popular competitive sport on Long Island.

Iceboating was a favorite pastime in the 1930s on Mill Neck Creek and provided a way for residents to enjoy boating in the winter months. Jack Davis's boat is the one with the star on the sail.

In June 1952, Paul Davis and Norman McCloy spent a day on the waters around Bayville. They proudly display their catch from a very successful blackfish fishing expedition.

This one-of-a-kind iceboat was built by Albert Schoverling. It was powered by a two-cylinder motorcycle engine. From left to right are Edward Shura, Rudolph Schoverling, and Quentin Schoverling.

Published in 1893, this song was written and composed by Frank F. Gray. Gray was a teacher and resident of Bayville who wrote it as a tribute to his hometown.

On this summer day at the Centre Island sound-side beach, the changing times are reflected in the various styles of clothing worn by the beachgoers as well as by the different modes of transportation parked along the road.

Lifeguards at Oak Neck Beach in 1955 from left to right are (first row) Hughie O'Hare, Art Yula, Tenn Burleson, George Famelle, Zeke Zowkowski, and Serge Nepo; (second row) Rudy ?, Bud Winslow, James Dougherty, Bill Winslow, and George Haefling.

An annual event at the fire company was the open house, when the trucks were pulled out of the garage and boots and hats were distributed to the youngsters who were allowed to climb on the trucks. Junior fireman Richard Cook hops on board a Bayville fire truck, as an unidentified youngster pretends to drive. Today the fire company holds an open house during Fire Prevention Week.

Village youngsters pose as firemen. Pictured are John Viteritti, Jack Valentine, Richard Cook, ? Strigaro, Robert Valentine, Dochie Tilford, Thomas Alfano, Charles Zeller, Francis Belsito, and George Viteritti.

Unidentified members and their fire department ball team junior mascot pose in front of the Bayville firehouse in this 1938 photograph.

In the 1970s, skating at the rink was a popular winter pastime. A fire to warm up by and a cup of hot cocoa were a welcome break during a fun day of skating.

Tucked behind the village hall complex, the skating rink doubled in the mild weather as a basketball court.

The Bayville Amusement Park's carousel was a favorite for the children of the village pictured here in the fall of 1962.

Ending a day at the beach, a trip to the amusement park was a special treat. In the background, the Oak Neck Beach bathhouse can be seen. The 1950s building is much different in style than the previous one, reflecting the more modern time.

Ferry Beach was a popular bathing spot for visitors and residents alike. With a bathhouse located at the base of the pier, people could walk off the ferry and spend the day at the beach. It later became Reinhard's Restaurant and Beach House. It is now the home of the Crescent Beach Club.

Many hot summer days were spent at this swimming pier that once stood just west of the Bayville bridge in Mill Neck Creek.

Seven

BUSINESS

William Flower started harvesting oysters in Mill Neck Creek in 1887. Today Frank M. Flower and Sons continues to be famous for Pine Island oysters. Many of the techniques of oyster and clam farming, including seeding, sowing, and harvesting, can be attributed to the Flower company. Shown is the Bayville hatchery on the Mill Neck Creek.

In 1925, Frank M. Flower and his three boys, Allen, Butler, and Roswell, built the *Ida May*. The boat is now at the waterfront center in Oyster Bay and is slated for restoration.

In the 1970s, these oyster company employees are hard at work. After a long day of harvesting oysters in the surrounding waters, they are sorting the harvest while heading in to their dock in Mill Neck Creek.

The Tilford family operated this blacksmith shop located at the end of the Bayville bridge on Ludlam Avenue. Blacksmiths in 1890 shoed horses and also made small tools, hardware, nails, and other building materials.

A mechanic at the Bayville branch of Dudley's garage assists a young couple with car trouble. Dudley's garage was conveniently located next to the Bayville Casino and across from the beach. It is not known where the other branches were located.

In 1940, traffic was moving steadily along Bayville Avenue on this busy afternoon in the village while this police officer was writing a parking ticket. In the background was the Great Atlantic and Pacific Tea Company grocery store, more commonly known as the A&P, one of the first grocery store chains.

At Friendly Corner at the intersection of Main Street and Lover's Lane, now Bayville Avenue and Perry Avenue, stood O. H. Perry's store. The area was known as Oak Neck and remained the village center until the first bridge to Oyster Bay was built at the east end of town.

This replica of the interior of Perry's store can be found inside the Bayville Historical Museum. The store had everything a family needed from dry goods, pottery, and household items to farming equipment.

ASPARAGUS FARMS IN BAYVILLE

John Bell began farming asparagus in 1825. The crop increased so dramatically over the years that Bayville farmers were shipping their produce to the New York markets daily. The industry slowly diminished when Bayville began to flourish as a summer resort community. The Bell farm was on the northeast side of Perry Avenue along with the Merritt farm. Nicholas Godfrey's farm was on the section now known as Bayville Park Boulevard.

Over the years, this structure built by Samuel Taylor in the 1920s has been home to multiple commercial establishments, including Abe's Stationery, a real estate office, an automobile service station, a physical fitness studio, a hair salon, and a Chinese restaurant.

Workers posing in front of Thos. Roulston market from left to right are W. Smith, J. Gallher, "Dad," G. Rost, and H. Bishop.

Our Hobby Market, located on the north side of Bayville Avenue at the intersection of Pine Park Avenue, was the local grocery store. The owner, Joseph Barnao, was an active member of the Bayville community whose efforts helped with the growth of the village. A yearly tradition at Christmastime was the Our Hobby Market pony pulling Santa's sleigh loaded with gifts for the neighborhood children.

A common daily sight in the 1940s was the pony Jack of Diamonds pulling the Our Hobby Market wagon. With the war on, the shortage of gasoline and rubber made the delivery wagon an alternative to the automobile. The market wagon could be seen in the village and on its way to Centre Island every day during this time.

OUR HOBBY MARKET
FROM A BITE TO A BANQUET
CENTER ISLAND ROAD
BAYVILLE, L. I., N. Y.

BILL OF SALE FOR EQUIPTMENT OF
THE CENTRE ISLAND BEACH NORTH SIDE +
southe side concession exapt

Such as: *wooden tables & chairs + Beer*
refrigaration on southe side

Refrigeration in cellar
Dressing room
All iron chairs and iron tables
Beach umbrellars and beach chairs
Pop corn machine
1 cash register
1 ice box
All kitchen equiptment that are on the premises

Amount $500
$250 paid in cash
$250 bal. to be paid on or before *Cept 15,* 1944

Also agreed by Mrs. Tagliabue to let Mr. Barnao
store wooden tables, wooden chairs and beer
refrigeration system on the south side.

Lillian Tagliabue

Joseph Barnao

In 1944, Joseph Barnao, the owner of Our Hobby Market, purchased equipment for the Centre Island Beach Snack Bar from Lillian Tagliabue.

When the small restaurant and snack bar concession was opened at Centre Island Beach, patrons stopped in for lunch or came up from the beach for an ice cream, a cold drink, or a snack.

Seated on the Shaffer Brewing Company delivery truck are Michael Murphy (left) and his brother Jack Murphy. Their father is in the white apron with three unidentified men.

Pictured in the 1930s behind the youngster in the wicker stroller is the barbershop and Tilford's Garage at Friendly Corner. Tilford's Garage was located here for many years before moving to its new building at Ludlam Avenue, which was constructed with lumber recycled from the old wooden bridge.

By the 1930s, the village center had started to shift from Friendly Corner to Bayville and Ludlam Avenues, as shown in this photograph.

Businesses along the intersection of Bayville and Ludlam Avenues in the 1950s included the Holiday Café, Moss's Drugstore, the A&P, and the Texaco gasoline station. The Holiday Café later was home to several different restaurants. The building was destroyed by fire in 2008. The drugstore space is currently home to a real estate office. The gasoline station property is now the village commons.

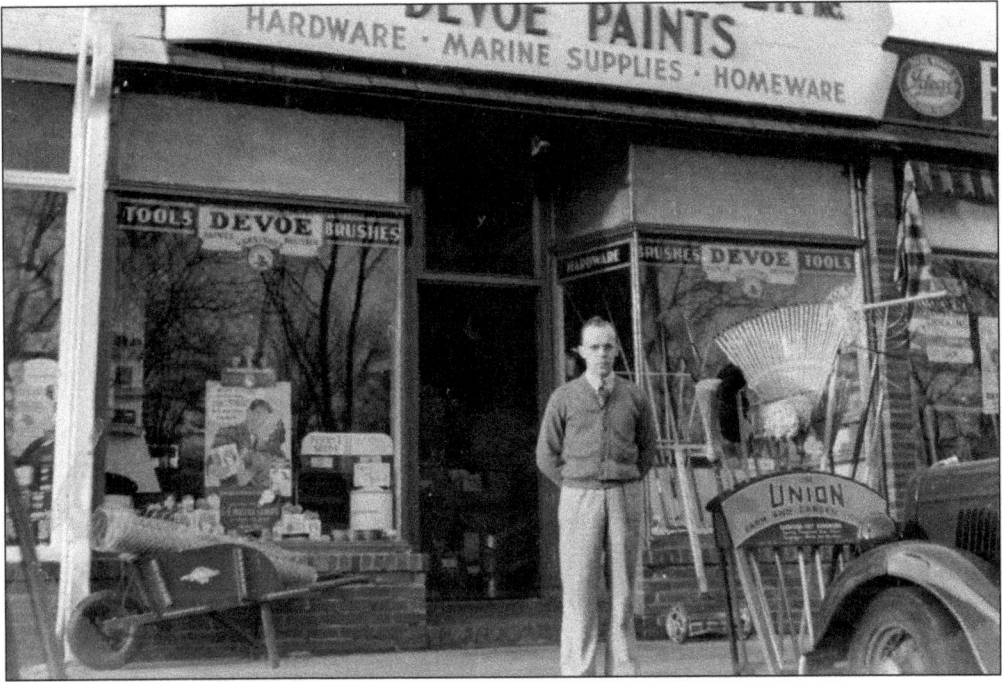

In the mid-1900s, Coombs and Oliver was a hardware store that offered a wide variety of merchandise, including nuts and bolts, sporting goods, boat supplies, fishing tackle, beach ware, bicycles, and paint.

This replica of the James Cowith Grist Mill was part of a Long Island Railroad exhibit at the New York 1964–1965 World's Fair. It was purchased by a real estate developer and brought to Bayville to coincide with the opening of the Northwind Shopping Center. It stood at the entrance to the center for many years until it was removed due to deterioration beyond repair.

The down side for out-of-town visitors in the winter months was that all the seasonal concession stands closed down in the off-season. This motorist discovers how lonely the beach area of the village is, especially after a snowstorm.

In the late 1940s, a group of friends are enjoying a walk in front of the Pig 'N Whistle, a popular restaurant across from the beach. Pictured from left to right are Rosalie Di Giovanni, James Di Giovanni, Angela Carbone, and Catherine Barnao Carbone.

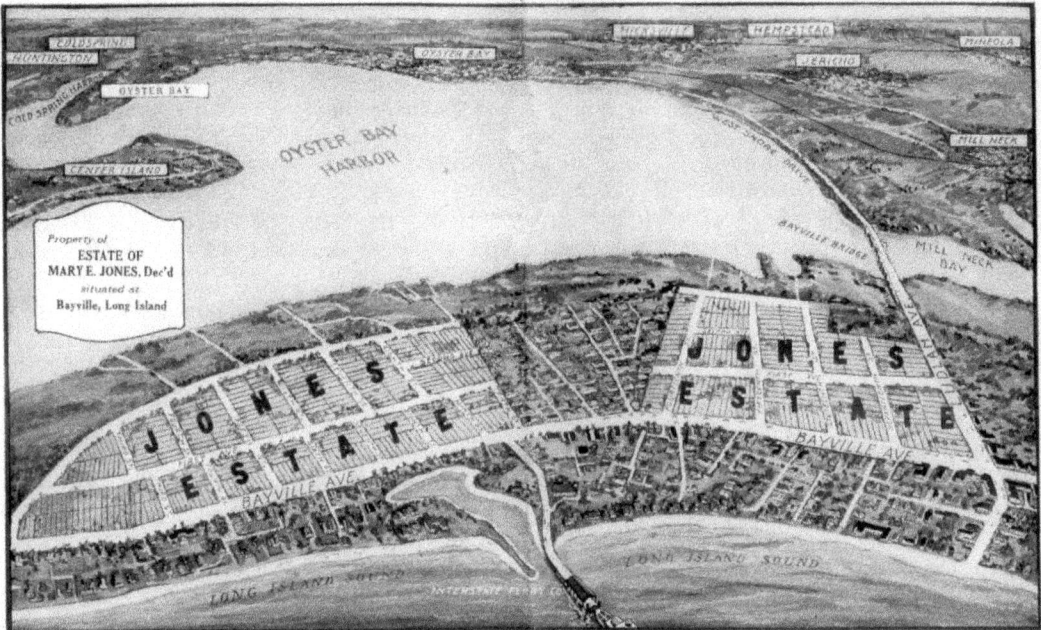

Dr. Oliver Livingston Jones and his wife, Mary, owned the large area of land known as Pine Island. Their daughter Rosalie, a leader of the suffrage movement, and her brother held a trustees auction upon the death of their parents. The acreage was divided into several hundred lots. The area stretched from Ludlam Avenue to Fourteenth Street and from Tenth Street to Third Street.

119

An Opportunity to Buy the Cream of North Shore

*H*ERE is great news for every one who is interested in the North Shore of Long Island, either from the standpoint of owning a seashore home or from that of making money. **THE PROPERTY OF THE MARY E. JONES ESTATE IN BAYVILLE, TOWN OF OYSTER BAY, LONG ISLAND, COMPRISING 792 BUSINESS AND BUNGALOW LOTS, IS TO BE OFFERED AT PUBLIC AUCTION ON AUGUST 7TH NEXT.**

Various sections along the North Shore have been opened up during the past year or so. Practically every offering made of Long Island North Shore real estate within commuting distance of New York City has been immediately absorbed and every one who has bought lots anywhere along the North Shore of Long Island in the early stages of development has made money rapidly and in surprisingly large amounts.

THE MOST POPULAR SEASHORE COMMUNITY ON THE ENTIRE NORTH SHORE OF LONG ISLAND WITHIN COMMUTING DISTANCE OF NEW YORK CITY IS BAYVILLE.

Bayville is a piece of woods and hills surrounded by water on three sides and directly adjoining that famous millionaires' colony, Center Island. No foolish restrictions have retarded the growth of Bayville. Lots near the water have been offered at reasonable prices, and literally thousands of summer and all-year bungalows and cottages have gone up in this vicinity during the past few years. Everything that has been offered in and around Bayville has been immediately snapped up by people who appreciated the advantages of this **RARE COMBINATION OF REAL COUNTRY AND SEASHORE.**

To meet the requirements of a summer colony that must number close to 10,000 people, business sections have been opened up along Bayville Avenue and West Shore Drive (Ludlam Avenue), the only streets in Bayville where it is practical to have business.

In each succeeding Bayville development higher prices were asked, but it seemed that no matter what prices were paid for the lots, those prices doubled, trebled, and even quadruped in a short space of time. **BUSINESS PROPERTY IN BAYVILLE HAS SOARED.** Property along Bayville Avenue and West Shore Drive (Ludlam Avenue) suitable for business is bringing hundreds of dollars a front foot.

It is no wonder that prospective home-owners and investors in Bayville and vicinity have always looked with longing eyes on the property owned by the Mary E. Jones Estate located right in the heart of Bayville's intensive development and containing the only remaining undeveloped business frontage in this popular bungalow community. It meets the needs of the thousands who live there now and of the probable hundred thousand population of the near future that will occupy every available foot of building space on every site within miles and miles of Bayville's wonderful beaches.

For seventy-five years the Mary E. Jones Estate has been held intact in one family, with the exception of a small parcel located right in the center of the lots to be offered, which section, known as Sound Beach, has been intensively developed with attractive summer homes. Bayville has had to build up all around the Mary E. Jones Estate. The builders of Bayville have had to skip the most desirable property within its limits. **THE MARY E. JONES ESTATE COMPRISES THE MOST DESIRABLE BUSINESS AND RESIDENTIAL PROPERTY IN ALL BAYVILLE.**

The tract to be offered at auction rises to a decided height above the shore line. It is covered with fine old trees, something that is rarely found so close to the seashore. Every lot to be offered is high and dry. And the Mary E. Jones Estate, as a whole, is probably as close to the water as any development that was ever offered. **EVERY BUILDING SITE IN THIS TREE-STUDDED PENINSULA OVERLOOKS AND IS LESS THAN 600 FEET FROM EITHER OYSTER BAY HARBOR OR LONG ISLAND SOUND.**

Owning a bungalow on the Mary E. Jones Estate in Bayville will be like living on a wooded island out at sea. Think of being able to buy an incomparable seashore location like this within an hour's commuting distance of New York! Think of being cooled by sea breezes all night long after a hot day's work in your office! Think of being able to purchase the last remaining vacant busines

---

For the 75 years prior to this auction, the land belonged to the Jones family. This was the sales brochure for the property. Each lot was within 600 feet of the Long Island Sound or Oyster Bay Harbor. The amenities of the community were extolled in this prospectus. Reasonable prices

usiness and Bungalow Lots at Your Own Price

New York, $10.84 to Brooklyn. Oyster Bay is the terminal of the branch of the Long Island Railroad that bears its name.

Oyster Bay has modern stores, schools, theatres and banks, and churches of all denominations. The schools are said to be as good as any on the Island. Oyster Bay has two newspapers and an excellent public library of many volumes.

THERE IS PRACTICALLY NO AVAILABLE UNDEVELOPED WATERFRONT RESIDENTIAL PROPERTY IN OYSTER BAY. The coming auction sale probably represents the last opportunity that the people of Oyster Bay will have to own desirable waterfront lots in the near vicinity of the village.

The Mill Neck Station of the Oyster Bay Division of the Long Island Railroad is still closer to Pine Island, the property to be sold, than is the Oyster Bay Station. In fact, it is within an easy walking distance of the propety. Mill Neck offers almost as many trains as Oyster Bay, and is still nearer to the city in point of time.

BUS LINES RUNNING ON AN HOURLY SCHEDULE CONNECT BAYVILLE WITH OYSTER BAY and also with Glen Cove, another well-known Long Island community. The busses pass directly in front of many of the business lots to be offered at the coming auction.

Thousands of people come over from Connecticut to bathe on the wonderful Bayville beaches. The ferry-boats from Rye and Greenwich, Conn., dock immediately opposite the center of Pine Island within a few hundred feet of some of the lots to be sold. These Connecticut ferries add to the TRAFFIC AND POPULATION that is helping to make Bayville the most popular recreation resort on the North Shore of Long Island.

There are a number of well-known Golf Clubs and Country Clubs in the immediate vicinity of Bayville. **CENTER ISLAND WITH ITS INTERNATIONALLY KNOWN SEAWANHAKA YACHT CLUB IS JUST ACROSS OYSTER BAY HARBOR, HARDLY A STONE'S THROW AWAY.**

Residents of Pine Island and Oyster Bay do not have to depend on the stores of Oyster Bay or their supplies because the business section of Bayville, directly across the street from many of the lots to be offered, will provide nearly all the supplies that the average family would require. The department stores of New York and Brooklyn make frequent deliveries to Bayville. There are many families who live the year round at Bayville, and the members of these families commute daily to New York.

Any location on the North Shore of Long Island at whatever price you may pay is a good buy when you consider that seashore property within commuting distance of New York City is being taken up with amazing rapidity, and when you stop to think that **THERE IS ROOM AT THE SEASHORE NEAR NEW YORK CITY FOR ONLY ONE-ONE HUNDREDTH OF NEW YORK CITY'S POPULATION.**

A seashore home will pay for itself over and over again in the form of health and happiness for yourself and your family. The law of supply and demand makes the purchase of seashore property within commuting distance of the city a safe and sound investment, promising big profits because the supply is almost exhausted and the demand is ever increasing. The purchase of lots anywhere in Bayville, the most popular bungalow community on Long Island's North Shore, is as sure to make money for you as any real estate that you could buy. And the Mary E. Jones Estate, with its incomparable location, every lot within 600 feet of the water, and surrounded by intensive development, represents the most remarkable summer home and investment opportunity that has been offered in many years.

When you buy Bayville residential and business lots from the Mary E. Jones Estate at prices far less than the prices of the surrounding lots, you will know that it will be only a short time before the Mary E. Jones Estate will be built up just as solidly as the rest of Bayville is built up all around that this ideally situated tract will soon be a thriving community of homes and stores like the rest Bayville, that future values will equal and eclipse the fancy prices that are now being paid for

made this a great opportunity to purchase land for a summer cottage or year-round home. This, along with an easy commute into Manhattan by either the Long Island Railroad or the ferry, made this offering attractive to many.

In May 1952, the groundbreaking ceremony for the construction of the Matinecock Bank building took place on Bayville Avenue east of Ludlam Avenue. From left to right are Winslow Valentine, Joseph Barnao, Joseph Geraghty, bank president Tom Bellingham (with shovel), and other unidentified officials. The bank borrowed its name from the Matinecock Indians.

Besides the Matinecock Bank, this newly constructed 1950s building also became the home of Twin Harbor Drugstore, which is now the Bayville Meat Market and the future home of First National Bank of Long Island.

This aerial view of the Stands in 1970 shows from left to right L'Epicure Restaurant, the Pig 'N Whistle, Soundview Motors, Gian Lorenzo's, Ralph's Pizza, Caldwell Realty, Souvlaki Place, and Soundview Marine.

In the 1920s, Ritzmore on the Sound was a popular spot on a summer's day for ice cream and cold drinks. In the evenings, it was a hot spot for dinner and dancing.

The North Shore Casino and Beer Garden, Bayville, Long Island, N. Y.

North Shore Casino and Beer Garden was another popular establishment with a full restaurant, informal cafeteria, and open-air outside beer garden. The building is now the home of Souvlaki Place and EVO Sport Fitness Club.

The Bayville bathhouse in 1927 was located on the west end of town across from what is now Ransom Beach. It later became a boat supply store. Since 1961, it has been the home of Ralph's Pizza.

124

On pleasant days at Ralph's Pizza in the 1970s, patrons were treated to open-air dining. The storefront had two large, glass roller doors that opened to views of the beach. The business has been family run for three generations.

Demolished in March 2009, Steve's Pier I was once a popular restaurant that was known for its beautiful nautical interior and breathtaking views of Long Island Sound. Visitors came by the busloads to enjoy a meal at this establishment.

An artist's rendition shows the bridge that Robert Moses proposed building across the Long Island Sound from Bayville to Rye. Part of Robert Moses's "Greater Plan," it was fought by area residents in the late 1960s and early 1970s. The creation of the Oyster Bay National Wildlife Refuge prevented its construction. The picturesque nature of the village was preserved, and the special qualities of life in Bayville continue to make it a place residents treasure.

BIBLIOGRAPHY

Grohman, Adam. *Non Liquet: The Bayville Submarine Mystery*. Self-published, 2006.

Hammond, John E. *Oyster Bay Remembered*. Huntington, NY: Maple Hill Press, 2002.

Mackay, Robert B., Anthony K. Baker, and Carol A. Traynor. *Long Island Country Houses and Their Architects, 1860–1940*. New York: W. W. Norton and Company, 1997.

Upright, Carlton B. *The Times and Tides of Bayville, Long Island, N.Y.* 1969.

Wycoff, Edith Hay. *The Fabled Past*. Port Washington, NY: Kennikat Press, 1978.

Visit us at
arcadiapublishing.com

....

www.ingramcontent.com/pod-product-compliance
Lightning Source LLC
Chambersburg PA
CBHW080558110426
42813CB00006B/1334